JERRY HELMS

HELMS
TO
HELLO

an Effective
Defense to 1NT

MASTER POINT PRESS • TORONTO, CANADA

Master Point Press
331 Douglas Ave.
Toronto, Ontario, Canada
M5M 1H2
(416) 781-0351

Websites:	www.masterpointpress.com
	www.teachbridge.com
	www.ebooksbridge.com
	www.bridgeblogging.com
Email:	info@masterpointpress.com

Library and Archives Canada Cataloguing in Publication

Helms, Jerry

Helms to HELLO : an effective defense to 1NT / written by Jerry Helms.

ISBN 1-897106-10-6
ISBN 978-1-897106-10-5

1. Contract bridge--Bidding.   I. Title.

| GV1282.4.H44 2006 | 795.41'52 | C2006-900080-8 |

Editor	Ray Lee
Cover and interior design	Olena S. Sullivan/New Mediatrix
Interior format	Suzanne Hocking

2 3 4 5 6 7   16 15 14 12

Contents

Thanks Gini and Big Jake.

HELMS

Many years ago (1974, to be exact), I modified a convention called Gladiator to use as a weapon to compete against opening notrump bids. Recognition that shape, suit length and quality are more important than high card strength, especially when competing after strong openings, led to the creation of the following convention.

HELMS[1]

2♣	Relay to 2◇. Shows a single-suited hand. Pass the forced response to show diamonds or convert to a major suit.
2◇	Both majors.
2♡	Hearts and an undisclosed minor. Advancer[2] uses 2NT to ask for the minor.
2♠	Spades and an undisclosed minor. Advancer uses 2NT to ask for the minor.
2NT	Both minors.
3♣	Clubs.
dbl	Penalty. More often based on tricks rather than just scattered high card strength.

Despite the immensely popular acceptance of this convention, a significant weakness seemed obvious, as illustrated by the following:

---

1. Fred Hamilton and Mike Cappelletti Sr. both claim to have originated this convention. Many people still refer to this treatment as Hamilton or Cappelletti.
2. *Bridge World* magazine suggested using the term "Advancer" to identify the player responding to overcalls or doubles. If it's good enough for them...

Hand 1	♠ K x x	**Hand 2**	♠ K Q J 10 x x
	♡ A J 10 x x x		♡ x
	◇ Q x x		◇ x x x x
	♣ x		♣ K x

On each of the hands above, the system bid of 2♣ allows the opponents the entire two-level to begin their exchange of information.

The problem, along with my solution, is documented by noted bridge author Max Hardy. "This convention ... loses the opportunity to block the opponents out of the auction which should be one of the goals of a bidder who holds a good major suit and hears an opening bid of one notrump by his right-hand opponent ... one theorist ... Jerry Helms took the problem into consideration and came up with a simple but effective solution. He interchanged the meanings of an immediate bid of two in a major suit and a bid of two clubs followed by a rebid in a major suit."[1]

> 'Constructive/obstructive' is the term I use to define my principle of competitive bidding: Describe your hand to partner while consuming as much of the opponents bidding space as possible. My first revision, HELMS II, was a movement in this direction.

---

1. *Competitive Bidding with Two Suited Hands* by Max Hardy, 1996, p117

HELMS II

HELMS II

2♣	Relay to 2♢. Confirm a natural diamond overcall by passing, or show a major/minor two-suiter by converting the forced diamond response to one of the majors. Advancer may use 2NT to discover the unknown minor.
2♢	Both majors.
2♡	Hearts.
2♠	Spades.
2NT	Both minors.
3♣	Clubs.
dbl	Penalty. More often based on tricks rather than just scattered high card strength.

Natural major-suit overcalls, as permitted in HELMS II, remedied the major fault of the previous system without sacrificing any positive attributes.

During the years that Jim Krekorian lived in Charlotte, we frequently discussed bridge theory, including improvements in HELMS II using transfer overcalls. The finishing touches of the original HELLO system evolved during the Jerry HELms and Bill LOhmann partnership. Perhaps HELKREKLO or some other variation would have been more appropriate, but...

HELLO
(Helms-Lohmann)

2♣	RELAY TO 2◊. Confirm a natural diamond overcall by passing or show a major/minor two-suiter by converting the forced diamond response to one of the majors. Advancer may use 2NT to discover the unknown minor.[1]
2◊	A transfer overcall to HEARTS.
2♡	BOTH MAJORS. Achieves transfer effect when Advancer chooses spades.
2♠	SPADES. A natural, space-consuming overcall.
2NT	A transfer overcall to CLUBS.
3♣	BOTH MINORS. Achieves transfer effect when the Advancer chooses diamonds.
3◊	BOTH MAJORS. Massive playing strength. The forced transfer eliminates the risk of a pass of 2♡ (both majors) by Advancer.
dbl	PENALTY. Most often based on tricks from a good suit. Occasionally a very strong, balanced hand.

---

1. I highly recommend an alternative suggested by Steve Weinstein. Advancer bids 3♣ as a pass or correct bid, with 2NT reserved as a 'heavy raise' of partner's now identified major suit.

HELLO is a unique convention providing options to describe all single- or two-suited hands without giving up penalty doubles of strong notrumps. The transfer effect achieved on many auctions may be, according to Bill Lohmann, the strongest part of the system. With the exception of 2♣ (diamonds or a major/minor), all suits are known. This information is important to permit raises by Advancer, and for opening lead considerations.

Recognition that being *in* the auction is generally better than being *out* of the auction can be summed up by the following:

> **LOOK FOR REASONS TO BID**
> **BEFORE FINDING EXCUSES**
> **TO PASS**

Using HELLO to apply the concept of 'constructive/obstructive' bidding should improve your results in competitive auctions.

The examples which follow assume equal vulnerability versus a strong notrump opening bid and are not intended to portray aggressive actions. Vulnerability, positional considerations and partnership sense of humor must always be considered. Always remember that guidelines will never replace judgment, and judgment in bridge comes only with experience. Enjoy yourself as you explore HELLO.

applying hello

W	N	E	S
			1NT
	?		

♠ xx
♡ xxx
◇ KQ1098x
♣ Kx

2♣   Passing the relay response confirms diamonds.

♠ AJxxx
♡ x
◇ xx
♣ KQ10xx

2♣   Convert the diamond relay response to 2♠, showing spades plus an unknown minor. By agreement, Advancer uses 2NT or 3♣ to ask for the minor.

♠ Kx
♡ AQJ10xx
◇ Jxx
♣ xx

2◇   A transfer overcall to hearts.

♠ Jx
♡ KQJ10x
◇ xxxxx
♣ A

2◇   A transfer overcall to hearts. With a suit this strong, best to emphasize what you really have.

♠ x
♡ KJ1098xx
◇ QJ10
♣ xx

3♡   Do not forget to use a natural preemptive bid.

♠ K10xxx ♡ J10xxxx ◇ x ♣ x	2♡	Both majors. 'Six-five, come alive!' is a useful bridge phrase when holding unbalanced hands.
♠ AKJxxx ♡ AQJ10xx ◇ — ♣ x	3◇	Both majors, massive playing strength. Bid game after partner's forced preference. 2♡, also both majors, could have been passed.
♠ AJ10xxx ♡ x ◇ KJ10x ♣ xx	2♠	Natural bids are encouraged.
♠ x ♡ xx ◇ Q10xx ♣ KQJ109x	2NT	A transfer overcall to clubs.
♠ x ♡ xx ◇ AQ10xx ♣ KQJ109	3♣	Both minors. The transfer effect will be achieved each time Advancer chooses diamonds.
♠ KJx ♡ AQx ◇ Kxx ♣ KJxx	pass	Facing a pure guess on opening lead versus 1NT doubled, simply pass.
♠ xx ♡ AKQJxxx ◇ xx ♣ xx	dbl	A 'fourth-best' lead will certainly defeat 1NT. Bid hearts when and if the opponents run.

♠ QJ109x   dbl

♡ AQ

◇ Kxx

♣ AJx

Not as secure as the prior example. With a clear opening lead and plenty of outside entries, take a chance.

♠ KQJ109xx   4♠

♡ —

◇ AQJxx

♣ x

Bid what you expect to make opposite virtually any dummy. Do not bid 2♠ or 3♠, or consider 2♣ to describe a two-suited hand. Give up on slam with a practical, space-consuming bid.

aDVancInG HeLLo

Shapely hands with good playing strength always provide a reason to bid. To encourage aggressive actions in the direct seat over notrump opening bids, Advancer needs to be somewhat conservative. In auctions where obstructive bidding is advisable, the first player to bid should be given the most rope. In other words, don't hang your partner!

Assume a strong notrump with equal vulnerability.

W	N	E	S
			1NT
2♣[1]	pass	?	

1. Relay to 2◊.

♠ Axx ♡ Jxxx ◊ x ♣ QJxxx	2◊	Accept the relay and await your fate. Perhaps partner has a major/minor or very good diamonds.
♠ x ♡ KJ10xxx ◊ xx ♣ Qxxx	2♡	A possible spade/diamond two-suiter by partner is a revolting thought. Failure to accept the relay is an attempt to play in your own suit. Partner is forewarned, but not barred, from further bidding.

W	N	E	S
			1NT
2♣[1]	pass	?	

1. Relay to 2◇.

♠ xxx	pass	A rare hand to justify this rare inaction. Partner may think you forgot the convention, however, the appearance of dummy may restore his confidence.
♡ xx		
◇ x		
♣ QJ10xxxx		

♠ Axxx	2NT[1]	The 'Heavy 2NT'. A massive acceptance for diamonds or the possible major/minor two-suiter. This is a useful conventional agreement to guarantee a fit and issue the strongest possible invitation to game.
♡ K10xx		
◇ Qxxx		
♣ x		

After the 'Heavy 2NT', partner can sign off in 3◇ with a minimum single suited diamond hand, or sign off in 3♡/3♠ with a minimum two-suiter. With a good hand he can simply jump to the appropriate game, secure in the knowledge that dummy will provide excellent supporting cards.

1. After any HELLO action, 2NT by the Advancer is always "fit-showing" and the strongest possible invitation to game.

W	N	E	S
			1NT
2◊¹	pass	?	

1. Transfer to hearts.

♠ Jxxx   2♡   Complete the transfer.
♡ xx
◊ Qxxxx
♣ Jx

♠ Ax   3♡   Mildly invitational. If partner
♡ xxxx   has a good hand, he may bid a
◊ Kxxxx   reasonable game. If he holds a
♣ xx   minimum shapely hand, your action
                             may preempt the opponents.

♠ xx   2NT   The 'Heavy 2NT' guarantees
♡ Axx   fitting cards. It is the
◊ AKJxx   strongest game invitation.
♣ xxx   Experienced partnerships may
                             wish to use 3◊/4◊ as a
                             retransfer to reject or accept.

♠ Axxxxx   4♡   Defending against a concealed
♡ Kxx   hand with unknown shape is
◊ AQx   difficult. The transfer effect
♣ x   also protects the diamond tenace
                             and forces an opening lead from
                             the strong hand.

W	N	E	S
			1NT
2◇[1]	pass	?	

1. Transfer to hearts.

♠ AJ10xxx   2♠

♡ x

◇ QJxx

♣ xx

An action suggesting lack of interest in hearts. If partner holds a good hand including a spade fit, game is still possible. 2NT by West would show a spade fit ... the 'Heavy 2NT'.

♠ xxx   pass

♡ x

◇ KQJ10xx

♣ xxx

A rare unilateral choice that may deprive partner from more bidding. Compare this decision with the 2♠ bid above which left partner involved.

♠ Qxxxx   2♡

♡ x

◇ Qxxxx

♣ Qx

Why speculate on a better fit? Occasionally partner will hold a very good suit or maybe the opponents will balance.

W	N	E	S
			1NT
2♡¹	pass	?	

1. Both majors.

♠ xx
♡ x
◇ Kxxxx
♣ Axxxx

2♠

The worst part is having to play the hand if partner has been overly aggressive (especially if the opponents double).

♠ Jxx
♡ Jxx
◇ Axxx
♣ Kxx

2♠

This will allow you to compete to the three-level by bidding hearts if the auction becomes competitive. If partner has been playing extremely well, consider passing 2♡.

♠ Qx
♡ Kxxx
◇ Kxxxx
♣ xx

3♡

Mildly invitational. As previously stated, this action may win by creating a maximum plus score or a minimum minus.

W	N	E	S
			1NT
2♡[1]	pass	?	

1. Both majors.

♠ Axxx **2NT**
♡ Kx
◇ xx
♣ KQxxx

Still another example of the 'Heavy 2NT'. The overcaller rejects with 3♡ or accepts with 4♡, both of which allow Advancer to pass or correct. Nice option, huh?

♠ AQ **4♡**
♡ AKxx
◇ xx
♣ xxxxx

Take a chance!

♠ xx **3NT**
♡ xx
◇ Kx
♣ AKQJ10xx

With seven sure tricks, focus on the good things that may happen with aggressive bidding. A good partner will recognize your total lack of major suit interest and provide a dummy with two tricks ... and a club to reach your hand!

W	N	E	S
			1NT
2NT[1]	pass	?	

1. Transfer to clubs.

♠ Axxxx	3♣	Shortness in partner's suit, outside defensive strength and a troubled pass by right hand opponent indicate danger. Bid 3♣ firmly and sound confident! Opponents who sense trouble are more likely to double.
♡ KQx		
◇ Jxxx		
♣ x		

♠ Axxx	bid clubs	LOTS of clubs. Depending on vulnerability and partner's sense of humor, bid 4♣ or 5♣.
♡ x		
◇ xxxx		
♣ Kxxx		

♠ xx	3◇	This hand could be a disaster for play in clubs. A diamond suit of this length and quality justifies the decision to refuse the transfer.
♡ xxx		
◇ AQJ109xx		
♣ x		

W	N	E	S
			1NT
3♣[1]	pass	?	

1. Both minors.

♠ AQxxx	pass	Confidently! Aggressive action will not always bring positive results. The good news is that partner plays this misfit.
♡ Q10xxx		
♢ x		
♣ xx		
♠ xxxx	3♢	Gain the transfer effect on this potentially very good bad hand. If the opponents do not lead trumps ...
♡ AJxxx		
♢ Kx		
♣ Qx		
♠ AKxxxx	6♢	This hand occurred to me in a vision late one evening – if twelve tricks are not possible in diamonds, my nocturnal partner's bidding needs a wake-up call.
♡ x		
♢ AJxx		
♣ Ax		

```
FACED WITH A PURE GUESS
ALWAYS GUESS HIGH —
THE REWARDS ARE GREATER
```

W	N	E	S
			1NT
3◇ [1]	pass	?	

1. Massive major two-suiter.

♠ xxx ♡ xx ◇ KJxx ♣ QJxx	3♠	A simple preference to one of partner's suits shows a bad hand opposite a very good one. On this auction, your minor-suit high cards are not carrying full weight.
♠ x ♡ Jxx ◇ Axxxx ♣ xxxx	4♡	3◇ shows a massive major two-suiter. Advancer should bid game with any excuse. Excuses: Three trumps, a singleton, an outside ace. A leap to 6♡ is a better estimate of the value of this hand than a mere 3♡ preference.
♠ xx ♡ x ◇ KQxxxxx ♣ xxx	3♠	Partner's strong action requires advancer to select a major-suit preference. The temptation to pass 3◇ is understandable, but do not yield, since partner may have game in hand.

Hardy-Inspired Adjuncts

EXCLUSION DOUBLES

The concept and value of using 'Exclusion Doubles' after interference over a 2♣ bid (HELLO, Helms, et al.) was identified clearly by Max Hardy in his excellent book *Competitive Bidding With Two Suited Hands*. My recommendations:

W	N	E	S
			1NT
2♣[1]	2X	dbl[2]	

1. Relay to 2◇.
2. Fit-showing, invitational.

Doubles by Advancer of any bid (up to and including 3♣) guarantee a fit for any of partner's hand types and suggest further competition. Logically, this means Advancer holds at least three cards in each of diamonds, hearts and spades.

♠ Q x x	♠ Q x x x	♠ A x x x
♡ x x x x	♡ J x x x	♡ A x x x
◇ A x x x	◇ K x x	◇ x x x x
♣ Q x	♣ x x	♣ x

On each of the above, Advancer should make an 'exclusion double' showing a desire to compete to the three-level opposite a diamond overcall or a major/minor two-suiter. This tool encourages the 2♣ bidder to continue bidding with the knowledge that partner has values and fitting cards.

W	N	E	S
			1NT
2♣[1]	2X/3♣	dbl[2]	pass
?			

1. Relay to 2◇.
2. 'Exclusion double', fit-showing.

- 3◇ confirms a diamond overcall.
- 3♡ confirms hearts and a minor.
- 3♠ confirms spades and a minor.
- Pass confirms your opinion that the opponents have erred by bidding one of your suits.

W	N	E	S
			1NT
2♣[1]	dbl	?	

1. Relay to 2◇.

- Redouble is 'exclusion', confirming a fit.
- Pass is neutral.
- 2◇ shows at least three diamonds.
- 2♡/2♠ is natural, usually a six-card or longer suit.

The use of Hardy-Inspired Exclusion Doubles and Redoubles are excellent additions to HELLO. I recommend them.

HELLO in THE PASSOUT SEAT

Successful penalty doubles of 1NT most often result from tricks taken in long suits. Doubling in fourth position and hoping that partner, on lead, will find your suit seems optimistic. Max Hardy suggested that a passout seat double of 1NT should request partner to bid 2♣. Pass confirms a club overcall. If corrected to another suit, it shows the following:

W	N	E	S
			1NT
pass	pass	dbl[1]	pass
2♣	pass	?	

1. Relay to 2♣.

♠ Kxx
♡ x
◇ Axx
♣ Q109xxx

pass

Allows you to compete in clubs at the two-level.

♠ Jxxxx
♡ Q
◇ AJxxx
♣ Kx

2◇

Diamonds and a major. Advancer passes with a diamond preference or bids 2♡ to ask for a major. 2NT is available as a heavy invite.

♠ Q10xx
♡ Axx
◇ KQxx
♣ xx

2◇

Diamonds and a major. This agreement provides an option for somewhat safer aggressive balancing actions.

♠ Kxxx
♡ Axxx
◇ Qxxxx
♣ —

2◇

Diamonds and a major. Gives you a three-way shot at finding your best fit.

W	N	E	S
			pass
1NT	pass	pass	dbl[1]
pass	2♣	pass	?

1. Relay to 2♣.

♠ KJxx   2♠   Spades and clubs. Implies
♡ xx   four spades, guarantees
◇ x   five or more clubs.
♣ A10xxxx

♠ Jx   2♡   Hearts and clubs. Implies
♡ Jxxxx   four hearts, guarantees five
◇ x   or more clubs. Looks like a
♣ AQxxx   four-card heart suit to me.

♠ Ax   pass   Clubs. With an immediate
♡ xxx   2NT also available to show
◇ Qx   clubs, this is the weaker
♣ Q10xxxx   sequence.

```
┌─────────────────────────────────────────────────┐
│                   A GOOD BID                      │
│   IS ONE THAT RESEMBLES THE CARDS YOU HOLD        │
└─────────────────────────────────────────────────┘
```

As previously noted, except for double, HELLO bids retain normal meanings in the passout seat. The following identifies a major/minor two-suiter with appropriate playing strength.

W	N	E	S
			1NT
pass	pass	2♣[1]	pass
2♦	pass	2♡/2♠	

1. Relay to 2♦.

♠ A x	♠ K J 10 x x
♡ Q J 10 x x	♡ x
◊ A J 10 x x	◊ A x
♣ x	♣ K J 10 9 x

Hands of less shape/strength are described by doubling then converting the forced 2♣ response.

If multiple meanings of double in passout seat seem complex, accept the fact that a passed hand double shows clubs, with 2NT an option to show more clubs.

W	N	E	S
			pass
1NT	pass	pass	dbl[1]
pass	3♣	pass	pass

1. Clubs.

♠ x
♡ K x x
◊ Q x x x
♣ A J 10 9 x

W	N	E	S
			pass
1NT	pass	pass	2NT[1]
pass	3♣	pass	pass

1. More clubs

♠ x
♡ Q J 10
◇ x x x
♣ K Q J 10 9 x

HELLO AFTER ULTRA-WEAK NOTRUMPS

Most players bold enough to use notrump ranges of 10-12 or 10-13 have extensive runout systems for escape after penalty doubles. Since these opponents tend to pass only with values and expectations of a plus score, penalty doubles on shapely hands tend to lose effectiveness. Direct or passout seat doubles of ultra-weak notrump openers are best used to imply strong, balanced hands. This agreement allows Advancer to treat the double as if his partner had opened a strong notrump. All normal partnership notrump systems then apply in or out of competition.

W	N	E	S
			1NT[1]
dbl	pass	?	

1. Ultra weak notrump.

East may use all normal notrump systems (Stayman, Transfer, etc.) just as if West had opened 1NT.

W	N	E	S
			1NT[1]
dbl	2X	?	

1. Ultra weak notrump.

East should have the same options he would have if West opened 1NT and North overcalled. Some form of Lebensohl is strongly recommended.

All other HELLO actions retain standard meanings.

Some partnerships choose to extend HELLO to cover all non-strong notrump opening bids.

HELLO afTeR NoTRump OveRcaLLs

Excellent results can be achieved using HELLO when partner's one-level suit opening bid is overcalled by 1NT.

W	N	E	S
			1♡
1NT	?		

♠ xx　　　　2◇　　　　　　A transfer raise of hearts,
♡ Kxxx　　　　　　　　　simple raise values.
◇ xx
♣ Qxxxx

♠ QJxxx　　2♡　　　　　　Both majors. At least three
♡ Kxx　　　　　　　　　　hearts plus five or more
◇ xx　　　　　　　　　　 spades. This information may
♣ xxx　　　　　　　　　　help opener in competitive partscore
　　　　　　　　　　　　　 battles.

♠ x　　　　　2♣　　　　　 Relay to 2◇. Either diamonds
♡ xx　　　　　　　　　　　or a major/minor. Plan to
◇ KJ10xxx　　　　　　　　pass the forced 2◇.
♣ J109x

♠ Q10x　　　2♣　　　　　 Relay to 2◇. Correct to 2♡ to
♡ xxxx　　　　　　　　　　show heart support plus a five-
◇ x　　　　　　　　　　　 card or longer minor. An
♣ KJxxx　　　　　　　　　indirect heart raise via 2◇ is the other
　　　　　　　　　　　　　 option.

W	N	E	S
			1♡
1NT	?		

♠ KJ10
♡ J10
◇ KQJxx
♣ xxx

dbl

Penalty, as always. This is the only strong action available.

♠ 1098xxx
♡ x
◇ QJ10x
♣ xx

2♠

With the master suit, strain to be in the auction. Failure to double denies a good hand.

♠ xx
♡ xx
◇ xx
♣ QJ10xxxx

2NT

A transfer overcall to 3♣.

♠ x
♡ x
◇ K1098x
♣ QJ9xxx

3♣

Both minors.

♠ xxxxx
♡ Qxxxx
◇ x
♣ xx

3♡

Preemptive. Bid at least 3♡, and depending on vulnerability and your partner's sense of humor, perhaps 4♡.

W	N	E	S
			1♣
1NT	?		

♠ AKQ10x
♡ xx
◇ Jxx
♣ Jxx

dbl

Penalty. Any shape. The only way to show 10+ high card points after right-hand opponent has overcalled 1NT.

♠ KQJ10x
♡ x
◇ xxxx
♣ xxx

2♠

Natural. Non-forcing. Failure to make a penalty double always denies a strong hand.

♠ KJ9xx
♡ Q10xxx
◇ xx
♣ x

2♡

Both majors.

♠ xxx
♡ AQ109xx
◇ xxx
♣ x

2◇

Transfer overcall to hearts.

♠ Axx
♡ —
◇ Jxxxxxx
♣ xxx

2♣

Relay to 2◇.

W	N	E	S
			1♣
1NT	?		

♠ xx
♡ x
◇ QJ109xxx
♣ J10x

3◇

Lots of diamonds. Illogical to use this as a strong major two-suiter.

♠ KJxxx
♡ x
◇ K109xx
♣ xx

2♣

Relay to 2◇. Follow with a 2♠ continuation, showing spades plus a minor. Opener 'runs' from spades with 2NT to ask for a minor.

♠ Jxx
♡ x
◇ Jxx
♣ xxxxxx

2NT

Clubs. Failure to double denies high card strength. Raising to the three-level in this auction suggests tricks.

♠ x
♡ xx
◇ AJ10xx
♣ J10xxx

3♣

Both minors.

♠ Q10x
♡ Jxx
◇ Q10xx
♣ QJ10

pass

More defense than offense.

general Defensive guidelines

The avoidance of complex methods to cope with all forms of interference may be desirable. The following simple defense for HELLO, or other systems interfering with your 1NT opening, is suggested.

'All Systems On' after all doubles. Redouble forces 2♣. Responder either passes or converts, showing a poor one-suited runout. Direct transfers to a major invite opener to compete further if necessary.

'All Systems On' after 2♣ interference, almost irrespective of its natural or conventional meaning. Double becomes Stayman.

Play Lebensohl around actual suit or suits shown, not the artificial bid heard.

If the interference specifies two suits, cuebid the suit you can stop. Invitational or stronger values.

Doubles of two-level natural bids are penalty.

Doubles of three-level natural bids are negative.

Doubles of artificial bids or relays are value showing, suggesting at least enough points for a 2NT raise. An alternative is to use doubles to show length.

'All Systems On' after 2NT interference:
3♣ = Stayman. 3◇/3♡ = Transfers.

W	N	E	S
			1NT
dbl	?		

♠ xx
♡ Jxxxx
◇ xxxx
♣ xx

redbl

After the forced 2♣, bid 2♡. This shows a woeful hand and pleads with opener not to compete if opponents bid.

♠ x
♡ KJ10xx
◇ J10xx
♣ xxx

2◇[1]

Transfer to hearts. Not invitational but, with fitting cards, opener is invited to raise in a competitive auction.

♠ xxxx
♡ xx
◇ xxxx
♣ xxx

pass

Quoting an old Motown favorite: "Nowhere to run, nowhere to hide."

♠ Q10x
♡ Axx
◇ 109xx
♣ Q10x

pass

If this double is for penalty, smile inwardly and pass. If the opponents run, double!

♠ AJxx
♡ Qx
◇ Kxxxx
♣ xx

2♣

Stayman. A penalty double is likely based on solid clubs or semi-solid hearts. If the double is conventional, do not allow their obstructive methods to interfere with your constructive methods.

---

1. Announced as a transfer.

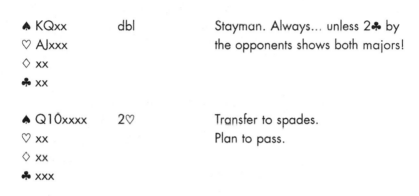

W	N	E	S
			1NT
2♣¹	?		

1. Relay to 2◇.

♠ KQxx	dbl	Stayman. Always... unless 2♣ by
♡ AJxxx		the opponents shows both majors!
◇ xx		
♣ xx		

♠ Q10xxxx	2♡	Transfer to spades.
♡ xx		Plan to pass.
◇ xx		
♣ xxx		

W	N	E	S
			1NT
2◇¹	?		

1. Transfer to 2♡.

♠ AQ10xx	2NT	Lebensohl around the heart
♡ xx		suit. Follow the forced 3♣
◇ Q10x		with an invitational 3♠.
♣ xxx		

♠ KJxx	2NT	Lebensohl. Follow the forced
♡ Ax		3♣ with 3♡. This 'slow' cuebid
◇ xxxx		is Stayman, showing a heart
♣ KQx		stopper. Lebensohl around the
		suit shown, not the suit bid.

W	N	E	S
			1NT
2♡¹	?		

1. Both majors.

♠ AQx ♡ xx ◊ xxx ♣ Q10xxx	2♠	Spade stopper with at least game invitational values.
♠ Ax ♡ KJx ◊ Kxxxx ♣ xxx	2NT	Lebensohl. After the forced 3♣, bid 3NT. Values for game. Both majors stopped. The 'slow' route to 3NT shows stoppers. 'Slow shows.'
♠ Jx ♡ xxx ◊ AKxx ♣ KJxx	3NT	Lebensohl. Values for game. No major-suit stoppers. The 'fast' route to 3NT denies stoppers. 'Fast denies.'

W	N	E	S
			1NT
3♡	?		

| ♠ Qxxx
♡ xx
◊ AJxx
♣ Axx | dbl | Negative. Penalty doubles based on trump tricks are unlikely after a three-level overcall of a strong 1NT. Opener may choose to convert to penalty by passing. |

HELLO AFTER STRONG OPENING BIDS

"The best defense against the strong, artificial ... opening ... is to open the bidding before your opponents can."

– C.C. Wei, Precision Club inventor

"The second best defense ... is to constructively/obstructively describe your hand to partner while consuming as much of the opponent's bidding space as possible."

– J. Helms, HELLO inventor

Once the opponents have opened the bidding artificially, negating the best defense, active intrusion is called for. Bidding theorists have long recognized that strong, artificial openings and their conventional responses may gain by identifying point values, but do so at the expense of specifying suits or distribution. To exploit this potential weakness, some modification of standard defensive methods is called for.

The late bridge expert Lew Mathe conventionally defined 'double' and '1NT' after a strong, artificial 1♣ opening or its negative diamond response as takeout for the majors and minors, respectively. By combining the straightforward and popular MATHE convention with modified HELLO, a more effective, defensive scheme may be employed.

HELLO/MATHE Strong Club

W	N	E	S
			1♣[1]
?			

1. Strong, artificial, forcing.

or

W	N	E	S
			1♣[1]
pass	1◇[2]	?	

1. Strong, artificial, forcing.
2. Artificial, usually negative.

pass   No suits, or a strong, balanced hand.

dbl   Both majors, 5-4 or weak 5-5.

1NT   Both minors, 5-4 or weak 5-5.

1◇/♡/♠   Natural, good suit, lead directive.

2♣   Transfer diamond preempt.

2◇   Transfer heart preempt.

2♡   Both majors, at least 5-5.

2♠   Spades.

2NT   Transfer club preempt.

3♣   Both minors, at least 5-5.

Using HELLO/MATHE, consider the following:

W	N	E	S
			1♣[1]
?			

1. Strong, artificial, forcing.

or

W	N	E	S
			1♣[1]
pass	1◊[2]	?	

1. Strong, artificial, forcing.
2. Artificial, usually negative.

♠ KJ10x	dbl	Both majors. Minimum
♡ KJxxx		playing strength.
◊ x		
♣ xxx		

♠ x	1NT	Both minors. Minimum
♡ xx		playing strength.
◊ Q10xxx		
♣ K10xxx		

♠ AQ109x	1♠	Obstruct the opponents by
♡ x		overcalling this strong suit.
◊ xxxx		
♣ xxx		

♠ AQ10	pass	The opponents are in a
♡ KJxx		forcing auction. Wait until
◊ AJxx		additional information is
♣ Kx		available.

W	N	E	S
			1♣[1]
?			

1. Strong, artificial, forcing.

or

W	N	E	S
			1♣[1]
pass	1◇[2]	?	

1. Strong, artificial, forcing.
2. Artificial, usually negative.

♠ x ♡ xx ◇ KJ10xxx ♣ Q10xx	2♣	A transfer to the diamond suit. Surrendering the dual major/minor option of 2♣ provides Advancer with a known suit.
♠ Jxx ♡ AJ10xxx ◇ xxx ♣ x	2◇	A transfer overcall to hearts.
♠ QJ10xx ♡ AQJxx ◇ xxx ♣ —	2♡	Both majors, at least 5-5. With less shape or texture, double is also available to show both majors.
♠ KQ10xxx ♡ x ◇ QJxx ♣ xx	2♠	Spades. At least 2♠. Consider your nerves, the vulnerability, partner's sense of humor, and make the maximum preempt.

W	N	E	S
			1♣[1]
?			

1. Strong, artificial, forcing.

or

W	N	E	S
			1♣[1]
pass	1◇[2]	?	

1. Strong, artificial, forcing.
2. Artificial, usually negative.

♠ xx ♡ x ◇ Kxx ♣ QJxxxxx	2NT	A transfer overcall to clubs.
♠ x ♡ x ◇ K109xxx ♣ AJ10xx	3♣	Both minors. At least 5-5 with good playing strength. 1NT is an option to express less strength/shape.
♠ — ♡ KQJ10xxx ◇ x ♣ QJ10xx	4♡	Don't confuse this with a two-suited hand.
♠ QJ10x ♡ — ◇ QJ10xxxx ♣ x	5◇	'Only' six high card points, however a ton of playing strength. Yes, partner could have spades. If so, unlucky!

By combining Mathe with a modified version of HELLO, your competitive options versus artificial club systems are expanded, and in my opinion, improved.

Summary of the options and their advantages:

Use Mathe at the one-level to imply less shapely two-suited hands with limited playing strength. Choose HELLO at the two-level to guarantee greater playing strength with at least 5-5 distribution. The certainty of the minimum total number of trumps is critical when Advancer attempts to apply 'The Law'.

Two-level preempts in diamonds and hearts, plus three-level club preempts all have the advantage of the transfer effect.

The immediate identity of the specific suit or suits shown by a conventional call provides the Advancer with an opportunity for maximum further preemption.

**BAD RESULTS FROM OVERBIDDING
NEVER SEEM AS PAINFUL AS
BAD RESULTS FROM UNDERBIDDING**

HELLO OVER A STRONG, ARTIFICIAL 2♣

Versus strong, artificial 2♣ opening bids, a modified style of HELLO can increase the opportunities and effectiveness of your constructive/obstructive options.

W	N	E	S
			2♣[1]
?			

1. Strong, artificial, forcing.

dbl	Transfer overcall to 2◊. Never two suits!
2◊	A transfer overcall to hearts.
2♡	Both majors.
2♠	Spades.
2NT	A transfer overcall to clubs.
3♣	Both minors.

W	N	E	S
			2♣[1]
pass	2◊[2]	?	

1. Strong, artificial, forcing.
2. Artificial, usually negative.

dbl	Both majors.
2NT	Both minors.

HELLO OVER A STRONG 2NT

Bidding over a strong 2NT opening suggests suicidal tendencies or very good playing strength. Consider using, with discretion, HELLO options as follows:

W	N	E	S
			2NT[1]
?			

1. Strong balanced hand.

dbl	A transfer overcall to clubs.
3♣	A transfer overcall to diamonds.
3♢	A transfer overcall to hearts.
3♡	Both majors.
3♠	Spades.
3NT	Both minors.

> IF YOU DON'T GET DOUBLED AND GO FOR
> A NUMBER OCCASIONALLY
> YOU ARE NOT BIDDING ENOUGH!

afterword

Helms to HELLO was originally published December, 1996, with no copies left by 2000. Over time, HELLO has been adopted by at least a few players all over the world. For the last few years, my Production Director, Penelope Smith has been encouraging me to the point of nagging to re-release the booklet. Procrastination has been a result of two factors: 1. For a man without a 'real job,' I am incredibly busy. 2. When speaking on my feet, my grammatical errors can often be turned into an entertaining plus. When I write, my need to be perfect borders on obsessive. A few errors in the 1996 edition, plus wording I felt could be better, kept me from simply ordering a reprint.

I am still busy; I still want each manuscript to be perfect, however, I finally couldn't stand explaining how I was working on a revision when actually all I was doing was thinking about working on a revision.

When applying HELLO, remember the following:

> **THINK AND THEN ACT**
> **RATHER THAN ACT AND THEN THINK**

As a matter of fact, this is an excellent guideline for most aspects of life.

Jerry Helms
November, 2005

About the Author

A successful bridge professional, Jerry Helms has turned his avocation into a full-time career. He specializes in large group seminars held primarily in resort areas. In addition, he is the author of the popular "Ask Jerry" columns in both the *ACBL Bulletin*, and *Better Bridge* magazine. His website is:

www.jerryhelms.com

For seminar information, email:

jerry@jerryhelms.com

With bridge questions:

askjerry@jerryhelms.com

CPSIA information can be obtained at www.ICGtesting.com
Printed in the USA
BVOW06s1600010216

435030BV00004B/9/P